AUSTRALIA
the people

Erinn Banting

A Bobbie Kalman Book

The Lands, Peoples, and Cultures Series

Crabtree Publishing Company

www.crabtreebooks.com

The Lands, Peoples, and Cultures Series

Created by Bobbie Kalman

Coordinating editor
Ellen Rodger

Project editor
Carrie Gleason

Production coordinator
Rosie Gowsell

Project development, photo research, design, and editing
First Folio Resource Group, Inc.
Erinn Banting
Tom Dart
Söğüt Y. Güleç
Claire Milne
Jaimie Nathan
Debbie Smith

Prepress and printing
Worzalla Publishing Company

Consultants
Jamie Breadmore; Amanda Burdon; Frank Povah, The Busy
Boordy; John Davison

Photographs
Tim Acker/AUSCAPE: p. 4 (top); Australia Tourism
Commission: p. 13 (right); Bill Bachman: p. 3, p. 16 (top),
p. 20 (top), p. 22 (right), p. 23 (bottom), p. 24 (top), p. 28
(both), p. 30 (both); Bill Bachman/Photo Researchers: p. 14
(top); Corbis/Magma Photo News, Inc./AFP: p. 11 (right);
Corbis/Magma Photo News, Inc./Bettmann: p. 26 (top);
Corbis/Magma Photo News, Inc./Matthew McKee, Eye
Ubiquitous: cover; Corbis/Magma Photo News, Inc./John
Noble: p. 6; Corbis/Magma Photo News, Inc./Reuters
NewMedia Inc.: title page, p. 13 (left), p. 25 (top); Corbis/
Magma Photo News, Inc./Paul A. Souders: p. 4 (bottom), p. 14
(bottom); Corbis/Magma Photo News, Inc./Penny Tweedie:
p. 12; Corbis/Magma Photo News, Inc./Michael S. Yamashita:
p. 8 (bottom); Marc Crabtree: p. 5 (top), p. 7 (top), p. 23 (top);
Paul Dymond: p. 15 (top), p. 18 (top); Jean-Paul Ferrero/
AUSCAPE: p. 16 (bottom), p. 17 (top), p. 24 (bottom), p. 27
(both); Gordon Gahan/Photo Researchers: p. 19 (left); David
Hancock-Skyscans/AUSCAPE: p. 19 (right), p. 29 (bottom);
Hulton/Archive by Getty Images: p. 8 (top), p. 9 (right), p. 11
(left); Hutchison Library/Liba Taylor: p. 15 (bottom); Jean-
Marc La Roque/AUSCAPE: p. 20–21 (bottom); Reg Morrison/
AUSCAPE: p. 5 (bottom); North Wind Pictures: p. 7 (bottom),
p. 9 (left), p. 10; Richard T. Nowitz: p. 17 (bottom); Chris
Sattleberger/Panos Pictures: p. 25 (bottom), p. 31; Mark
Spencer/AUSCAPE: p. 26 (bottom); SuperStock, Inc.: p. 22
(left); Penny Tweedie/Panos Pictures: p. 18 (bottom), p. 21
(top); Ulrike Welsch: p. 29 (top)

Illustrations
Dianne Eastman: icon
David Wysotski, Allure Illustrations: back cover

Cover: An Aboriginal woman from the Kakadu region, in the
north, prepares for a celebration known as a *corroboree*. During
corroborees, Aboriginals paint their faces in colors and patterns
that represent the person, animal, or event they are celebrating.

Title page: Surfing, scuba diving, snorkeling, and other water
sports are very popular in Australia.

Icon: A football, which is used in Australia's most popular
sport, Aussie rules football, appears at the head of each
section. These footballs are larger and rounder than footballs
in North America.

Back cover: When baby kangaroos, or joeys, are born, they are
the size of a bean. Joeys spend 33 weeks inside their mother's
pouch, by which time they are too large to be carried around.

Published by
Crabtree Publishing Company

PMB 16A,
350 Fifth Avenue
Suite 3308
New York
N.Y. 10118

612 Welland Avenue
St. Catharines
Ontario, Canada
L2M 5V6

73 Lime Walk
Headington
Oxford OX3 7AD
United Kingdom

Cataloging in Publication Data
Banting, Erinn.
  Australia. The people / Erinn Banting.
    p. cm. -- (Lands, peoples, and cultures series)
Includes index.
Summary: Explores how the history, climate, and geography
of Australia have shaped the customs and practices of its
people, looking at life in both the city and the Outback.
  ISBN 0-7787-9344-3 (RLB) -- ISBN 0-7787-9712-0 (pbk.)
  1. Australia--Social life and customs--Juvenile literature. [1.
Australia--Social life and customs.] I. Title. II. Series.
  DU107 .B37 2003
  994--dc21
                                                 2002013730
                                                 LC

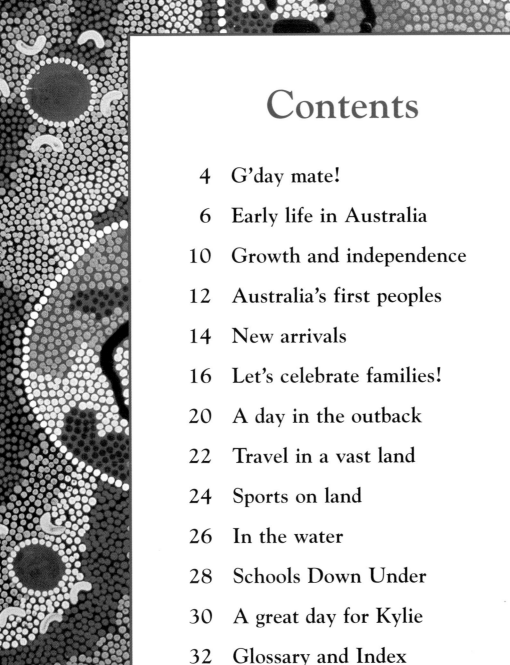

Contents

"G'day mate!" is the Australian way of saying "Hello!" to a friend. This greeting can be heard in busy cities, as neighbors bump into one another on their way to work or school, and on crowded beaches, where people gather to swim, surf, or have barbecues. In the hot, dusty outback, however, you can travel for long stretches without seeing anyone. This desert area, which covers two-thirds of the country, is home to only 20 percent of the population. The other 80 percent live mainly along or near the coasts, in the capital cities of Australia's six states and two main territories — New South Wales, Victoria, Queensland, Western Australia, South Australia, Tasmania, the Northern Territory, and the Australian Capital Territory.

Farmers proudly display their harvest of oranges on their farm near Sydney, in the east.

Sometimes, kangaroos make their way out of the outback and into populated areas, such as this golf course in the southeastern state of Victoria.

Most of Australia has a warm, sunny climate all year, so people spend a lot of time on the beach, even at Christmas!

Two boys display the ininti seeds they picked near Mount Liebig, in the Northern Territory. Some Aboriginals use ininti seeds, which come from bat-winged coral trees, to make jewelry, decorate baskets, or make collages.

Early life in Australia

Hundreds of millions of years ago, before humans existed, dinosaurs roamed Australia. At that time, Australia was closer to Antarctica, the coldest place on earth, and polar dinosaurs lived in the cool south. Unlike other dinosaurs, polar dinosaurs could survive the cold temperatures. **Fossils** of polar dinosaurs, such as the pterosaur, one of the few dinosaurs that could fly, have been discovered at a site called Dinosaur Cove.

The Aboriginals' arrival

The earliest known humans in Australia, the Aboriginals, arrived more than 60,000 years ago from Asia. Some Aboriginal groups lived in the outback and led nomadic lifestyles, traveling from place to place within their own territory in search of food and water. Other Aboriginal groups lived along the east coast, where there was more vegetation, or plants for food. These groups stayed in one place, occasionally leaving to hunt. Aboriginal groups in the southeast, in the present-day state of Victoria, were even more settled. They lived in stone houses and caught fish using traps.

Torres Strait Islanders

Almost 10,000 years ago, another group of people arrived in Australia and settled on the islands off the northeast coast, in the Torres Strait. The Torres Strait Islanders, as they came to be known, were from New Guinea, an island in the Pacific Ocean.

The first visitors

The Aboriginals and Torres Strait Islanders lived in Australia for thousands of years before people from other countries arrived on its shores. One of the earliest known visitors was Cheng Ho, a Chinese explorer in the 1400s. As early as the 1500s, the Macassans, from present-day Indonesia, had camps along parts of Australia's northern coast, where they fished and traded with Aboriginal people for part of the year.

These fossilized dinosaur footprints, which are hundreds of millions of years old, were discovered near Broome, a town in Western Australia.

European explorers

In the 1600s, European explorers began to come to Australia. Willem Jansz, a Dutch trader and **navigator**, landed there in 1606. Abel Janszoon Tasman, the Dutch explorer for whom the state of Tasmania was named, and William Dampier, a pirate and navigator from England, soon followed. What they found was a rugged land that did not look like it bore many riches. European interest in Australia increased in the 1770s, after an English explorer named James Cook landed on the east coast, in a lush, **fertile** bay, which he named Botany Bay. Cook explored the rest of the southeast coast until he reached the island of Tasmania, claiming both the continent and the island for Britain.

Penal colonies

During the 1700s, crime in England and Ireland increased because of poor living conditions. British jails became overcrowded and the government was forced to send its prisoners to **penal colonies** in the United States, which was ruled by Britain at the time. After the United States won its independence from Britain at the end of the American Revolution (1775–1783), the British government had to find a new place for its prisoners. It chose Australia.

On January 26, 1788, the first group of convicts, soldiers, and prison guards landed in Port Jackson, now Sydney Harbor, in the southeast. The leader of the group, Captain Arthur Phillip, became the governor of New South Wales, the first colony in Australia to be governed by the British. The convicts were sentenced to hard labor, farming the land and building homes and government buildings for the new British **colony**. Australia remained a penal colony for 80 years. In that time, 160,000 convicts were sent there.

This statue of Captain James Cook stands in the city of Perth, on the west coast.

Before the arrival of Europeans, some Aboriginal groups were nomadic, traveling within their own territory. Their territories were eventually taken over by the colonists.

NORFOLK ISLAND.—THE CONVICT SYSTEM.

Prisoners from a penal colony build a bridge on Norfolk Island, off Australia's east coast, in this illustration from the 1800s.

Free settlers

Starting in the 1830s, free settlers came to Australia from countries such as England, Ireland, Scotland, and Germany. Many of these settlers, who did not have legal rights to the lands on which they settled, became known as squatters.

Squatters and freed convicts who were trying to start farms soon discovered that tools, **livestock**, and labor were expensive and difficult to find. Eventually, some squatters were given long-term **leases** for the land they occupied, and many became very wealthy. Most freed convicts remained poor farmers or became bushrangers. Bushrangers made their living by stealing horses, cattle, and sheep from squatters and hiding out in remote parts of the country.

The impact of the British

The British established their penal colonies and settlements on land belonging to the Aboriginals and Torres Strait Islanders. Many Aboriginals and Torres Strait Islanders were killed in battles defending their land, or from diseases brought by the British. Many of those who were not killed were captured by the colonists and forced to work for them under terrible conditions.

Port Arthur, a penal colony in Tasmania, was where convicts who committed more crimes after being released from prison, were sent. Before it was closed in 1853, more than 30,000 convicts were sent there. The conditions in the gaols, or jails, where they lived were brutal and prisoners were often tortured. Many of the penal colony's buildings still stand as a reminder of the island's past.

Some Aboriginal groups, such as the Tasmanian Aboriginals, were almost entirely wiped out at the time of British and European settlement. Truganini, who was once believed to be the last Tasmanian Aboriginal, fought to protect her people and secure land for them to live on.

Burke and Wills' Expedition

As demand for new grazing land for livestock grew, settlers were forced to venture away from the coasts to Australia's interior. Explorers, such as Robert Burke and William Wills, were sent to find new land and a route between the northern and southern coasts. Burke and Wills' expedition was doomed from the start. They packed too heavily, refused to take an Aboriginal guide, and traveled during the hottest time of the year. Burke and Wills never completed their expedition. Having unloaded some of their supplies along the way, they died of starvation in the outback.

Burke, Wills, and a member of their party try to find their way in the outback, in this illustration from the late 1800s.

The Myall Creek Massacre

By the mid 1800s, the treatment of Australia's Aboriginals and Torres Strait Islanders worsened. Aboriginals and Torres Strait Islanders faced **discrimination**, and many were tortured and murdered. During the Myall Creek Massacre, in 1838, a group of English settlers murdered 28 Aboriginals. Some people say that the massacre took place because the English settlers thought the Aboriginals had stolen their cattle. Others say that the Aboriginals had killed several English shepherds and hutkeepers, who guarded the huts where convicts lived. The Myall Creek Massacre was the only massacre of Aboriginals in which the English were punished — seven of the eleven Englishmen involved in the incident were convicted of murder and were hanged.

Growth and independence

Gold was discovered in Australia in 1851. Stories about gold nuggets that weighed 200 pounds (91 kilograms) inspired people in Australia to leave their jobs and search for gold. People from as far away as the United States, China, England, Poland, and other parts of Europe sold their homes, farms, and possessions and moved to Australia to find their fortune. During the gold rush, 700,000 people came to Australia, tripling the population.

The Eureka Stockade

Competition and the high price of mining licenses caused tension in the goldfields. As tensions grew, miners began to protest and some even burned their licenses. On December 3, 1854, a **rebellion** broke out at the Eureka goldfield in Ballarat, Victoria. The rebellion was called the Eureka Stockade because approximately 150 miners, or diggers as they are called in Australia, built a stockade, or barricade, to keep out the police and soldiers who were sent to stop the uprising. Twenty-two diggers and five soldiers were killed during the uprising. Although people lost their lives, the rebellion was successful. Gold licenses were replaced by diggers' "rights," which cost less and gave the diggers more freedom.

In this illustration of a goldfield from the 1850s, men are sluicing, or washing gold from sand and dirt.

The Commonwealth of Australia

Australia's new wealth from gold, as well as a growing wool industry and the building of railroads, increased trade between colonies, making Australia more **self-sufficient**. With this new feeling of independence, some Australians wanted to govern their own country. In 1897, colonists accepted a new **constitution** which supported partial independence from Britain. On January 1, 1901, a new federal government was established.

The former colonies became states, and the country became the Commonwealth of Australia. Australia had the power to make its own decisions about trade, **immigration**, and defense, but England still controlled its relations with other countries. Canberra, in the east, became Australia's capital in 1913.

World War I

During World War I (1914–1918), Australian and New Zealand armed forces joined to create the Australian and New Zealand Army Corps, or ANZAC. The ANZACs were the only army made up entirely of volunteers. Of the 520,000 people from Australia and New Zealand who fought in support of England and its **allies**, more than 75,000 were killed.

On April 25, 1915, ANZAC troops stormed Gallipoli, a peninsula in Turkey, in an attempt to end Turkey's participation in World War I. The eight-month campaign, in which British, French, and Indian forces also participated, failed, and Britain and its allies were forced to evacuate. More than 8,000 Australian soldiers were killed, but were highly respected by other countries for their bravery in battle.

Australia today

In 1986, Australia became a constitutional monarchy, which means that the Queen of England is Australia's queen, but she holds no real power. Australia's federal and state governments make all the political decisions. In 1999, a **referendum** was held to decide whether Australia should become a republic. As a republic, Australia would have no ties to England. Supporters of the republic lost the referendum, but the debate continues as to whether Australia should maintain its link with England.

Malcom Turnbull, the head of the Australian Republican Movement (ARM), campaigns in Sydney before the referendum in this photograph from 1999. The ARM is a group that supports Australia's independence from England.

World War II

During World War II (1939–1945), the Australian Imperial Force (AIF) was formed to fight alongside England. In 1942, Japan, which at the time controlled much of Southeast Asia, took 15,000 Australian troops prisoner in Singapore. On February 19, 1942, Japanese planes bombed Darwin, a city in Australia's north. The bombs destroyed many buildings, sunk eight ships in the harbor, and killed or wounded nearly 600 Australians. Over the next three years, Australian and American soldiers fought against the Japanese in the Pacific, leading to the end of Japanese control of the region.

Immigration

By the time World War II ended in 1945, Australia's manufacturing and mining industries were growing. The government began to encourage immigration to increase the number of workers in the country. **Refugees** came from countries such as Germany, Hungary, England, Italy, and Greece. By 1972, more than four million people had come to Australia. Since 1973, Australia has also welcomed immigrants from countries such as China, Malaysia, the Philippines, Turkey, and Iran.

There were once more than 400 groups of Australian Aboriginals, each with its own territory, traditions, beliefs, and language. These groups included the Mara, Turrbal, Mirning, Kariera, and Bindubi. The Wiradjuri, who live in New South Wales, is one of the largest groups of Aboriginals today.

Respect for the land

Some of today's Aboriginals live a nomadic lifestyle, as their ancestors did, but two thirds of all Aboriginals live in cities and towns. They share a deep respect for the land. This respect comes from the fact that Aboriginals have traditionally depended on nature for their survival.

The Dreaming

The Dreaming is central to Aboriginal culture. The Dreaming consists of stories about the Aboriginals' ancestors. These ancestors created plants, animals, humans, and the laws of people and nature during the Dreamtime, which is when Aboriginals believe the world was created. The spirits of the ancestors still live in the landscape. They give energy to nature and guide humans in their everyday lives. Each person and Aboriginal group is connected to Dreamtime beings. They care for the land where these beings reside by performing ceremonies and singing songs that tell of the Dreamtime.

Aboriginal rights

Since the English arrived, the Aboriginals have struggled for their right to own their land, which they consider **sacred**. Beginning in the 1860s, many Aboriginals were moved from their land to reserves that were run by the government or by **missionaries**. On reserves, many Aboriginals were forbidden to practice their customs, they lost all their legal rights, and their children were taken away from them. Little improved until 1967, when Aboriginals were granted the right to vote and were included in the national **census**. Today,

there are no longer reserves. Since the 1970s, Aboriginals have been returning to their homelands, which are their traditional lands. Homelands are managed by Aboriginals or by churches on behalf of Aboriginals, and are given some money by the Australian government for health care, education, and other programs.

A crowd demonstrates for Aboriginal rights at the Australian bicentennial celebrations in Sydney in 1988. The celebrations marked the 200-year anniversary of the arrival of the British in Australia. Most Australians want their government to formally apologize to Aboriginal people for wrongs done to them since the British arrived. This is called the Reconciliation Movement.

The Mabo Decision

The Mabo Decision, which was passed in 1992, acknowledged that people lived in Australia before the British arrived. Earlier documents said that the land was uninhabited, and Aboriginals' claims to the land were constantly refused. In 1993, the Native Title Act was passed. It stated that if land was found to belong to an Aboriginal people, the government would help them buy it back. Farmers and miners who owned disputed land could make claims as to why they should keep it. Many rulings permit farmers and miners to keep the land, but allow Aboriginals to use it for religious ceremonies.

Famous Aboriginals

Conditions are improving for some Aboriginals, but most still do not have good jobs or decent living conditions. Some famous Aboriginals have used their high profiles to educate people about Aboriginal cultures and to fight for **equality**. Fred Maynard (1879–1944) was a well-known **activist** who demanded that Aboriginals be given the right to vote, own land, and be considered Australian citizens. Albert Namatjira (1902–1959) was a world-famous artist who gave the money he earned from his paintings to his people. Evonne Goolagong Cawley (1951–) is a tennis player who won many international tournaments. She faced a lot of discrimination, but her success changed many people's views about Aboriginal women.

Torres Strait Islanders

About half the Torres Strait Islanders in Australia make their living by fishing and farming in the Torres Strait. The other half live on the mainland, either in cities or on homelands. They speak two main languages — Kala Lagaw Ya and Meriam Mir. Torres Strait Islanders are distinct from Aboriginals, with their own customs and traditions, but there are similarities between the two peoples. For example, although most Torres Strait Islanders are now Christian, their traditional religion, Bipotaim, honors the past and shows respect for the land, just as the Aboriginal belief in the Dreaming does.

Girls wearing colorful grass skirts and headdresses made from flowers dance at the Torres Strait Cultural Festival, on Thursday Island. The festival is held every other year to celebrate the culture of the Torres Strait Islanders.

Aboriginal sprinter Cathy Freeman participates in the opening ceremonies of the 2000 Summer Olympics, in Sydney. She later went on to win the gold medal in the 400-meter sprint. The Olympics brought worldwide attention to the struggles of Aboriginals.

New arrivals

For a country its size, "the Land Down Under," as Australia is nicknamed, has one of the smallest populations in the world. The majority of Australians are descended from the English, Scottish, and Irish settlers who began arriving in 1788. Their methods for farming and for manufacturing textiles, and their stories, art, music, and foods, became part of everyday life in Australia. English dishes, such as fish and chips, are sold at restaurants or by street vendors throughout the country. Australian folk songs are often played with English, Irish, and Scottish instruments, such as the pan flute and bodhran, a type of drum.

(right) Greek dancers prepare to perform at a festival in Melbourne which celebrates Greece's Independence Day.

(top) European settlers introduced many animals to Australia, including sheep and rabbits. Today, Australia has ten times more sheep than people.

People from all over

Since 1940, Australia has become home to people from Lebanon, Yugoslavia, Hungary, Germany, Brazil, and other parts of the world. They introduced many of their traditions to the rest of the country. Italian, Greek, and Chinese food are all popular in Australia. Sydney's Chinese New Year celebrations, which begin on the first full moon in January, are enjoyed by people from all over the country. Melbourne's Greek Antipodes Festival, in March and April, is another lively celebration with traditional Greek music, dance, theater, film, and arts and crafts. The festival, whose name means "Down Under" in Greek, celebrates the blending of Greek and Australian cultures.

"White Australia" policy

During the gold rush, Australians, British, and Europeans working in the goldfields began to resent immigrants from Asian countries because many were willing to work for lower wages. This made competition for jobs fierce. As a result, Asians faced a lot of discrimination. In 1901, the Australian government implemented a "White Australia" policy to restrict immigration. Anyone who wanted to settle permanently in Australia had to take a **dictation** test in a European language. If potential immigrants, such as the Chinese or Japanese, could not speak whichever language was chosen for the test, they were not allowed in the country. The "White Australia" policy finally ended in 1973. Today, Australia welcomes immigrants from all over. It also trades goods with countries such as Japan, Taiwan, Singapore, and Malaysia. This trade has strengthened ties between the countries.

A teenager plays peek-a-boo with his baby cousin at a park in Cairns, a city in the east.

This woman and her family own a vineyard in southern Australia. Australia is one of the world's largest producers of wine.

Let's celebrate families!

Australian barbecues, or "barbies," are a lot of fun, especially when they are part of a special celebration, such as a birthday or anniversary. On these occasions, family and friends get together to play games, sing songs, dance, and enjoy each other's company.

Happy birthday to you!

Children in Australia have birthday parties like those in North America. Family and friends open presents and eat birthday cake and other treats. Children play games, such as Pin the Tail on the Donkey, Musical Chairs, and Pass the Parcel. To play Pass the Parcel, children in a circle pass a large parcel from one person to another while music plays. Each time the music stops, the child holding the parcel removes one layer of wrapping paper, until finally all the layers are gone and the lucky winner finds a small gift or treat inside.

Australian children enjoy treats, such as chocolate teddy bears, fairy bread, and "lollies," or candy, at their birthday parties. Chocolate teddy bears are types of cookies, and fairy bread is buttered white bread covered with multicolored sprinkles, called "hundreds and thousands."

A family shares a picnic at a park in Vaucluse, a city in New South Wales.

Three cousins have fun with their uncle at a wave pool at the Wylie Baths, a seawater pool in Sydney.

Turning 21

Turning 21 is an important event in Australia. It is considered the age when a person reaches adulthood. A huge party, with dinner, dancing, and toasts, is part of the fun. As a special gift, the birthday person sometimes receives a key, which symbolizes the key that opens the door to a bright future. Some keys are several feet tall, and open to reveal birthday wishes written on small pieces of paper.

Weddings in Australia are much the same as they are in North America, with a ceremony and a reception where family and friends celebrate with the bride and groom.

An Aboriginal boy performs a traditional dance at a **corroboree** *in Queensland.*

Corroborees and feasts

Corroborees are ceremonies that Aboriginals perform to celebrate stages in a person's life, such as birth, marriage, and becoming an **elder**. *Corroborees* usually include singing and dancing, but each Aboriginal group also has its own traditions, many of which are known only to elders. For example, at some *corroborees*, elders reveal stories about the Dreamtime that are depicted on large stones or boards called *tjuringa*. The Torres Strait Islanders have similar celebrations for special occasions, but they are called feasts. As with *corroborees*, people get together to sing, dance, and enjoy a large meal. The Torres Strait Islanders' meal usually consists of a green turtle or a **dugong**. These animals are caught in the waters around the Torres Strait Islands.

During **corroborees**, *people paint their bodies with patterns that usually represent their spiritual ancestors. Elders, who often lead* **corroborees**, *paint their bodies white and yellow. People being initiated are usually painted red.*

Initiation ceremonies

Aboriginal boys and men passing into a new stage of life face grueling rituals. Boys' initiation ceremonies, which mark their entry into adulthood, vary from group to group. Some initiations begin when the boys are thirteen and last several months. During that time, the boys must pass tests to prove that they can survive on their own in the wilderness. They are also taught about their ancestors' history. At the end of the initiation period, the boys are scarred at a special *corroboree*. The scars are a source of pride because they represent the pain that the boys endured. Girls are also initiated, but they do not go through the same trials as boys.

Celebrating the Dreamtime

Corroborees also celebrate a group's Dreamtime being. Each Aboriginal group has traditions to honor its creature. For example, the Arrernte, from central Australia, honor their Dreamtime being, the snake, with *pmara kutatja*, which are songs that sometimes take weeks to perform. The Yanuwa, from the Northern Territory, honor the brolga, a large crane. During a special ritual known as the *kulyukulyu*, or brolga dance, they paint their bodies and wear long straw wigs that look like the brolga's feathers.

Big history songs

Different songs are sung at different *corroborees*, depending on which creature is being honored. Sacred ceremonial songs called *kujika* are believed to have been handed down by the Dreamtime creatures. In English, these songs are called "big history songs" because some of them are more than 200 verses long.

Aboriginal people in the Northern Territory perform a dance to honor their group's totem, which is an emu. A totem is believed to protect a group from harm. During the dance, the performers make movements and noises that are like those of the large, flightless bird.

Pukumani poles, which are made from logs that have been carved and painted, surround a burial site on Bathurst Island, in the north.

Aboriginal funerals

Death is considered the most important passage in an Aboriginal person's life because it is believed that he or she returns to the Dreamtime. Aboriginal groups in the central-west part of New South Wales **mummified** and then buried the bones of important elders in a cave or in a hollow in the ground. Intricate carvings, called dendroglyphs, were made in tree trunks to mark the grave. Many Aboriginal peoples hold a smoking ceremony to cleanse a room after someone dies. They create the smoke for the ceremony by burning wet leaves in a small fire. According to some traditions, it is considered taboo, or wrong, to speak the name of the person who died for several days or months after the death. Some groups consider it taboo to say the person's name for ten years.

19

A day in the outback

Early explorers who came to the outback called it "the dead heart." The outback's rich, red soil looked like blood because of all the **iron** in it, and the vast land was so still and barren that it seemed lifeless. The outback is the largest and most remote part of Australia, made up of dry, sandy deserts and rocky land where there is little vegetation and few streams and rivers. Some Aboriginals leading a traditional way of life and farmers who live on large farms called sheep or cattle stations live in the outback, even though it is so rugged.

Outback towns

During the gold rush of the 1850s, thousands of people came to the outback in search of gold. Today, countless abandoned mines and eerie ghost towns serve as a reminder of that prosperous time. Many towns in the outback are very small and have only a general store, gas station, motel, and hall, where parties are held for special occasions. Farmers on cattle or sheep stations make the trip to town once a week to buy groceries and other supplies.

Shops and restaurants line a street in Charters Towers, which was the largest settlement in north Queensland during the gold rush.

Travelers on camels approach a hotel and rest stop in Silverton, a town in the outback.

The Flying Doctor

People in the outback sometimes live hundreds of miles away from the nearest doctor. The Royal Flying Doctor Service, which was started in 1928, provides people in these remote regions with medical care. Doctors and nurses are flown to people's homes and to community health centers. If patients are very ill, they are then flown to the nearest hospital. People can also contact doctors over radios to ask questions and receive medical advice.

Technology in the outback

Parts of the outback are so remote that people have to talk with one another using two-way radios because there are no telephone lines. In other parts, two-way radios are being replaced with telephones and Internet connections.

Videoconferencing, which allows people to communicate via satellite using video cameras, televisions, and telephones, is another way people can see and talk with one another. The Warlpiri, a group of Aboriginals in the Tanami Desert, in the Northern Territory, run a videoconferencing network. The network links several remote Warlpiri settlements with one another and with videoconferencing sites in Sydney, Darwin, and Alice Springs, which is in the middle of the outback. The Warlpiri use the network to talk with family members, hold religious ceremonies, study together, speak with doctors, display their artwork, and communicate with people in other countries.

To cross Australia, from Sydney on the east coast to Perth on the west coast, takes three days by train and an entire week by car. Parts of the trip are scenic, with views of the ocean and forests, but in other parts, the highway seems to go on for miles without anything interesting to see.

Big structures

Breaking up the landscape along some Australian highways are about 60 "big" structures, such as the Big Lobster, Big Koala, Big Lawn Mower, Big Orange, and Big Merino Ram. These painted structures, made from chicken wire and fiberglass, often represent something that is important to a region. The Big Lobster, for example, in Kingston, South Australia, is home to a restaurant that sells lobster caught locally. The first "big" structure was the Big Banana, at Coffs Harbor in New South Wales. Designed by an American named John Landi, it is 36 feet (11 meters) long and 16 feet (5 meters) high. It is surrounded by a banana theme park, which used to be a plantation called Horticultural World.

It is not uncommon to see kangaroo crossing signs along the roads in Australia's outback. Can you tell which other animals these signs are warning drivers to look out for?

Part of the Big Merino Ram in Goulburn, New South Wales, is a gift shop. Many of the farms in and around Goulburn raise Merino sheep, whose fleece is made into wool.

The Ghan

One-humped camels, called dromedaries, live in the western and central deserts of Australia. The dromedaries were brought to Australia from Afghanistan in the 1840s. They were used by the Ghans, the name given to the Afghan drivers who transported supplies to cattle and sheep stations in the outback. The dromedaries could withstand the hot, dry conditions of the desert. Then, in 1878, construction of a railroad track began. Today, a train, also called the Ghan, runs along the track that some of the camels once traveled, from Adelaide to Alice Springs.

The "Tea and Sugar"

The Trans-Australian Railway is a 297-mile-(478-kilometer-) long railway line that runs through the Nullarbor Plain, a desert that links South Australia to Western Australia. Until 1996, a train nicknamed "the Tea and Sugar" ran along this track once a week, providing supplies to people in small towns along the track and to workers who lived in camps and maintained the track. On the train was a butcher car; a provision shop car, which sold tea, sugar, coffee, bread, fruit, vegetables, drinks, and candy; and a car where people could pick up cleaning products, home decorations, and other household items that they had ordered. Dentists, doctors, nurses, and clergy traveled on the train to visit people living along its route, and a theater car sometimes showed movies.

Rough travel

Harsh weather, such as flooding and sandstorms often destroy the outback's unpaved roads, making travel to distant towns possible only in a four-wheel-drive vehicle. The Birdsville Track runs through a remote part of Queensland. People driving on this road to see the plants and animals of the outback must inform police before they go, so that search parties can be sent out in case travelers do not arrive at their destinations. The area is so remote that cell phones cannot pick up signals, and people cannot call for help if they need to.

(right) As cars and trains made travel faster and easier, the Ghans and their camels were no longer needed, and the camels were set free. Today, few people use camels for outback travel.

(below) Enormous road trains speed across Australia, carrying goods from place to place. Road trains are actually transport trucks that have a series of "dogs," or trailers, attached to one another. A road train can transport more than 1,000 sheep or hundreds of cattle at a time.

 # Sports on land

Australia's warm climate makes it a great place for outdoor sports and activities, such as golf, tennis, soccer, and cycling. More adventurous people go on bushwalking tours, where they camp and hike in the outback.

Come play cricket!

English settlers brought the game of cricket to Australia. Cricket is similar to baseball. A batter, called a striker, stands in front of a wicket. A wicket is made of three poles, with two bars on top. A bowler, who is like a pitcher, stands in front of another wicket 66 feet (20 meters) away. Beside the bowler is a runner, called a nonstriker, from the striker's team. The bowler bowls the ball, trying to knock down the wicket near the striker. The striker tries to keep the ball from the wicket by hitting it with a flat bat. If the striker succeeds, he and the nonstriker run between the wickets as many times as possible before a fielder returns the ball. Their team scores a run each time they switch positions. The team with the most runs at the end of the game wins.

(top) A striker runs to the opposite wicket in a cricket match in Melbourne.

Rugby is a very rough game, and players, who are not allowed to wear a lot of protective equipment, often get injured.

Rugby

What do you get when you cross football with soccer? You get a fast-paced game called rugby. In rugby, players kick and pass a ball, called a bladder, to their teammates. The ball can never be thrown or kicked forward. It can only be passed to the side or backward. To score a try, which is like a touchdown, a player has to touch the ball to the ground behind the H-shaped goal posts. To score a goal, or field goal, a player must kick the ball over the crossbar.

Australian rules football

In 1858, an Australian man named H.C.A. Harrison invented a game called Australian rules football. The game combines Gaelic football, which comes from Ireland and Scotland, with rugby. Aussie rules football, or "footie," is the most popular sport in the country. Two teams of eighteen players each try to score goals by kicking an oval ball through the goal posts at either end of the field. Players can pass the ball by kicking or handballing it, which means that they hold the ball in one hand and hit it with a clenched fist with the other hand. Throwing the ball is not allowed, and if players run with the ball, they must touch it to the ground once every 49 feet (15 meters). Aussie rules football is very rough and wild. Sometimes, it looks like the players are not following any rules at all!

A jockey urges his horse on as it nears the finish line of the Melbourne Cup.

Thousands of fans watch the final game of the Aussie rules football season, an event which is as popular as the Super Bowl in the United States.

And they're off!

The Melbourne Cup is held every year on the first Tuesday in November. It is the largest horse race in the country. The Melbourne Cup is so popular that it has been made an official holiday in the state of Victoria, where Melbourne is located, because so many people go to the race or watch it on television.

A different sort of race is held in Alice Springs. In the Camel Cup, which is held on the second Saturday in July, jockeys race camels instead of horses around a track.

In the early 1900s, twelve-year-old Alec Wickham, who lived on Solomon Island, north of mainland Australia, invented an arm-over-arm swimming stroke that looked as if he was crawling through the water. It became known as the Australian crawl. Today's front crawl is based on the Australian crawl. Swimming is still popular in Australia as are other water sports, such as surfing, scuba diving, and snorkeling.

Surfing

Off the beaches of Australia, surfers "hop on their sticks and catch a wave," which means they get on their surfboards and go surfing. They "catch a wave" by paddling out into the water while lying on their surfboard, and then they wait for a wave to roll toward shore. At just the right moment, they stand up on the board and "ride the wave," or surf, back to the beach.

In 1983, Australia shocked the world by winning the America's Cup, a sailing race held in the United States. By winning the race, the team, which sailed the Australian II, broke the United States' 132-year winning streak.

Snorkeling and scuba diving are great ways to see the beautiful marine life in Australia, especially on the Great Barrier Reef.

Surf lifesaving

Surf lifesavers use surfboards, skis, rubber dinghies with motors, and surf reels to save people caught in the ocean's strong tides. One end of a surf reel is attached by a rope to a heavy barrel on the beach. A surf lifesaver swims out to the person in trouble with the other end. Then, both the person in trouble and the surf lifesaver hold onto the reel, while another surf lifesaver pulls them in to safety.

Surf carnivals

It is not all work for surf lifesavers. Each summer, thousands of lifesavers participate in surf carnivals, where they have fun and show off their skills in competitions. The carnival begins with a "march past," in which twelve members from each surf lifesaving club march in formation to music with their reels, lines, belts, and club's flag. The toughest competition is the Ironman or Ironwoman competition. The race involves running, swimming, surf skiing, and board paddling. In surf skiing, surf skiers paddle long, narrow fiberglass boats, which look like kayaks, out into the waves. Once there, they try to keep their boats from tipping over. In board paddling, the contestants kneel on surfboards and paddle around buoys in the water.

At surf carnivals, lifesavers demonstrate their skills with rescue tools, such as reels, lines, and belts.

A surf boat crashes over the waves during a surf carnival off the Gold Coast, in Queensland. In surf boat rowing races, crews race in row boats to a marker in the ocean and then back to shore.

Schools Down Under

The school year in Australia is different from that in North America. It begins in January or February, and ends in mid December. Vacations in April, July, and October are two weeks long. The summer vacation, which begins in December, usually lasts for six weeks.

Different classes

Besides studying subjects such as English, math, geography, science, art, and music, some Australian students take surfing classes in school. Others learn to sail or get their motor boat license. In marine education, students learn about the plant and animal life in Australia's oceans. It is important for children to learn about marine life so that, when they are playing in the water, they can recognize and stay away from dangerous sea animals.

Students examine the plant and animal life in a pond during a "water watch" class.

Children act out a play about the five senses — sight, smell, touch, hearing, and taste — for their classmates at a school in the Tamami Desert, in the Northern Territory.

Great games

At recess, Australian children enjoy playing games such as Fizzy or Flippers. To play Fizzy, children stand in a circle. One child in the center of the circle throws a ball into the air. When he or she yells "Fizzy," the other children try to catch the ball. The child who catches the ball becomes "it" and moves to the center of the circle. Flippers is similar to hackey-sack. Children standing in a circle bounce a tennis ball to one another using their knees and ankles. Anyone who touches the ball with their hands or lets the ball outside the circle is out.

Schools of the Air

Children in the outback do not always live near a school. Some children go to boarding schools in cities and towns. Many others have a room in their house where they study, with a desk, bookshelf, maps, chalkboard, two-way radio, and computer. They participate in a School of the Air.

In a School of the Air, children spend half an hour each day on a two-way radio, listening to their teacher, having discussions with other students, and working on projects in groups — all with people who are far away. Private lessons with their teacher, which usually last ten minutes a day, are another part of the school program. The rest of the program is done through television, computer, e-mail, and regular mail. Children spend five or six hours each day doing schoolwork, then they send their work to their teacher to be marked. The oldest School of the Air is based in Alice Springs. Students who "attend" that school live in an area that covers more than 468,000 square miles (1,212,120 square kilometers).

A student on a sheep station in Western Australia reads a presentation he wrote about dinosaurs to his teacher and classmates over a two-way radio. Dinosaur fossils, which give scientists clues about what life was like millions of years ago, have been found in many parts of Australia.

When the student finishes his presentation, his teacher and classmates ask him questions about his project.

A great day for Kylie

Kylie plays with her uncle's puppies. When they grow up, the puppies will herd sheep at the station.

Kylie's uncle counts the sheep that have been sheared. Though shearing does not hurt the sheep, they sometimes get scared and run away.

Kylie and her parents had been driving through the outback for hours. They had taken a five-hour flight from Sydney, where they lived, to Perth, in Western Australia. From Perth, they had to drive another seven hours to get to Kylie's aunt and uncle's sheep station.

The outback was a lot different than Sydney. The office towers and paved roads were long gone. The only town they passed through had just a gas station, a general store, and a small motel. Otherwise, Kylie saw only red sandy deserts, a few trees and low bushes, and a farmhouse or two.

When they finally got to the sheep station, Kylie's cousin, Wes, ran outside and gave her a big hug. "Good to see you, mate! Dad and I are just on our way to check on the sheep. Want a tour of the station?"

Kylie jumped at the chance, and her uncle helped her climb into his four-wheel-drive truck. "Buckle up! It's a bumpy ride."

Wes, Kylie, and her uncle drove along a dirt road that circled the grazing area where the sheep munched away at shrubs and grasses. "There's not a lot of water out here in the outback," her uncle explained. "That's why we have so much land for so few sheep."

Riding on her motorcycle, Emily brings an injured sheep back to the barn, where she will examine it.

Kylie noticed some people in the distance. "Who are they?" she asked. "Oh," laughed her uncle. "That's Michael, Paul, and Emily. They work on the station tending to the sheep."

"They can shear all the wool off a sheep in one go!" Wes said in an impressed tone.

When they got home, Wes took Kylie inside to show her his bedroom and the room where he studied. Wes was in year six, a year ahead of Kylie.

"You go to school here?" Kylie asked. "Sure do," Wes replied. "My lessons are sent to me by e-mail or on videocassette. I also talk to my teacher and class on that two-way radio over there."

Just then, Kylie's aunt called out, "Barbie's ready, you two!" Wes and Kylie ran to the kitchen. Kylie couldn't wait to eat the delicious chicken, beef steak, **prawns**, and vegetables that her aunt and uncle had barbecued over a large grill.

After supper, Kylie's uncle turned on the television to watch the Aussie rules football match. Kylie and Wes cheered as Sydney's team scored another goal, putting them six points ahead of Melbourne's team.

When the game was over, Kylie's uncle called her outside. "Look at this," he said. Kylie gasped as she peered at the horizon. The setting sun had turned a beautiful pink color. "The whole station looks pink — even the sheep!" Kylie exclaimed. She was very glad that she had come to the outback.

Glossary

activist A person who works to change other people's ideas and actions about an important cause

allies A group of countries that help and protect one another

census The official count of a country's population

colony An area controlled by a distant country

constitution A set of rules, laws, or customs of a government or other institution

dictation The process of saying or reading something aloud for another person to write down

discrimination The act of treating people unfairly because of race, religion, gender, or other factors

dugong A large sea mammal, also called a sea cow

elder An older member of a family or community who is very respected

equality The state of everyone having the same rights and privileges

fertile Able to produce abundant crops or vegetation

fossil The ancient remains of animals or plants preserved in rock

immigration The process of moving to another country

iron A metal used to make tools and machinery

lease A contract that allows someone to occupy a property in exchange for rent

livestock Farm animals

missionary A person who travels to another country to spread a religion

mummified Preserved from decay

navigator A person in charge of steering a ship

penal colony A place in another country where criminals are sent for punishment

prawn An edible crustacean similar to shrimp

rebellion An uprising against a person or group in power

referendum The process of having citizens vote to approve or reject a law

refugee A person who leaves his or her home or country because of danger

sacred Having special religious significance

self-sufficient Able to look after or support oneself without help

Index

1 2 3 4 5 6 7 8 9 0   Printed in the USA   0 9 8 7 6 5 4 3 2